S0-ARN-317

Native Peoples of THE NORTHEAST

By Barbara M. Linde

Gareth Stevens
PUBLISHING

Please visit our website, www.garethstevens.com. For a free color catalog of all our high-quality books, call toll free 1-800-542-2595 or fax 1-877-542-2596.

Library of Congress Cataloging-in-Publication Data

Names: Linde, Barbara M., author.
Title: Native peoples of the Northeast / Barbara M. Linde.
Description: New York : Gareth Stevens Publishing, 2017. | Series: Native
  peoples of North America | Includes index.
Identifiers: LCCN 2015051114 | ISBN 9781482448269 (pbk.) | ISBN 9781482448139 (library bound) | ISBN
9781482447620 (6 pack)
Subjects: LCSH: Indians of North America–Northeastern
  States–History–Juvenile literature.
Classification: LCC E78.E2 L56 2017 | DDC 974.004/97–dc23
LC record available at http://lccn.loc.gov/2015051114
First Edition

Published in 2017 by
Gareth Stevens Publishing
111 East 14th Street, Suite 349
New York, NY 10003

Designer: Samantha DeMartin
Editor: Kristen Nelson

Photo credits: Series art AlexTanya/Shutterstock.com; cover, p. 1 Print Collector/Hulton Archive/Getty Images;
p. 5 (main) Christopher Hall/Shutterstock.com; p. 5 (map) AlexCovarrubias/Wikimedia Commons; pp. 7, 11 (main)
Nativestock.com/Marilyn Angel Wynn/Native Stock/Getty Images; p. 9 MPI/Archive Photos/Getty Images; p. 11 (inset)
stoonn/Shutterstock.com; p. 13 MPI/Hulton Fine Art Collection/Getty Images; p. 15 courtesy of Library of Congress;
pp. 17, 25 Kean Collection/Archive Photos/Getty Images; p. 19 Archive Photos/Archive Photos/Getty Images;
p. 21 Universal History Archive/Universal Images Group/Getty Images; p. 23 JTB Photo/Universal Images Group/
Getty Images; p. 27 Boston Globe/Boston Globe/Getty Images; p. 29 Gigillo83/Wikimedia Commons.

Printed in the United States of America

CPSIA compliance information: Batch #CS16GS: For further information contact Gareth Stevens, New York, New York at 1-800-542-2595.

CONTENTS

Words in the glossary appear in **bold** type the first time they are used in the text.

The NORTHEAST

Native peoples lived in the northeastern part of North America for over 12,000 years before European settlers arrived. Their lands **stretched** from the Atlantic Ocean to around the Mississippi River. They reached from the Great Lakes **region** all the way to the present-day state of Maine to the north.

Archaeologists think there were about 2 million native peoples living in the Northeast during the 1500s. It's believed they came to the Northeast from southwestern North America, but no one is totally sure.

This map shows that the native peoples of the Northeast lived in the present-day states of New York, Massachusetts, Ohio, Pennsylvania, and more.

Greenland

Canada

United States

Mexico

= where native peoples of the Northeast lived

TELL ME MORE

Before European settlement, much of the Northeast was covered with thick forests. So the native peoples are often called the Woodland Indians.

At Home in the NORTHEAST

Some of the native peoples of the Northeast lived in large groups with thousands of members and many villages. Other groups were smaller and didn't have **permanent** settlements. One kind of home found in the Northeast was the **dome**-shaped wigwam, also called a wickiup. Wigwams were made of wooden poles, grass, tree bark, and sometimes animal skins. Usually, just one family lived in a wigwam.

The rectangle-shaped longhouse was also made of wood. It had a door at each end. A longhouse could hold as many as 10 families.

The homes of the native peoples of the Northeast were easy to build and take down. This allowed groups to move with the seasons to hunt and gather what they needed.

TELL ME MORE

In many native languages, the word "wig" meant "to live in." The word "wigwam" means "their home."

Leader of the BAND

Native peoples in the Northeast are commonly grouped together by language or customs. Some groups had a main governing body. A chief and often a village **council** led most groups.

Though groups were set up differently, men and women had similar duties in each. Men were warriors and hunters. Women made clothes, farmed, cooked, and took care of the family. Boys and girls learned their place in the community from the adults.

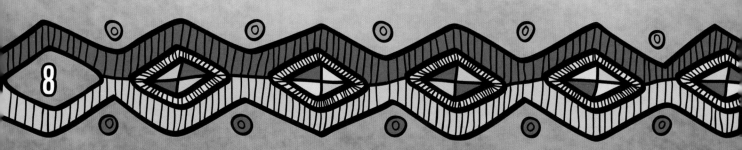

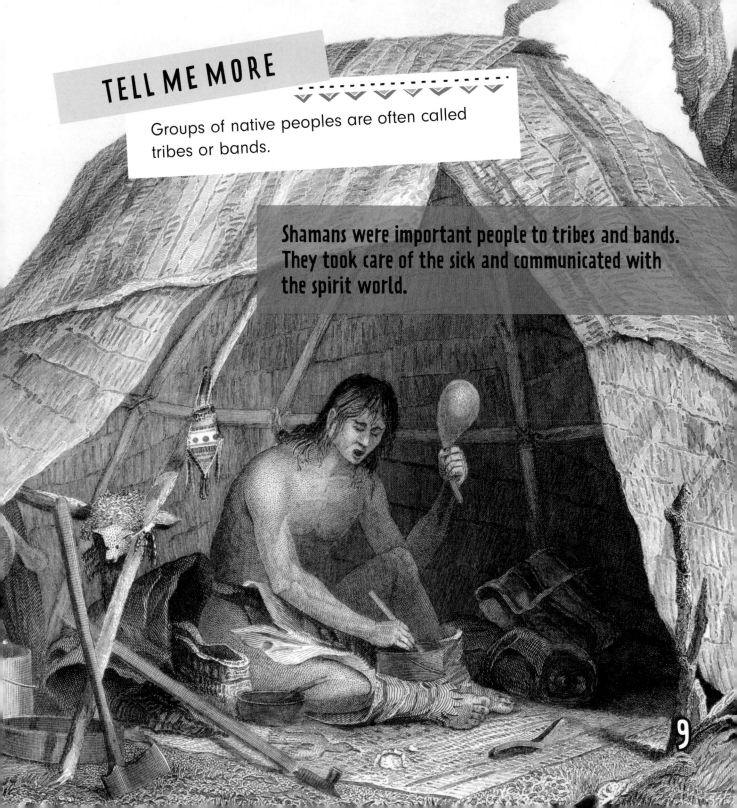

Groups of native peoples are often called tribes or bands.

Shamans were important people to tribes and bands. They took care of the sick and communicated with the spirit world.

What to EAT?

The northeastern region of North America includes woodlands, the Atlantic coast, meadows, and more. Because of the many **environments**, what native peoples ate depended on where they lived. Most groups hunted animals, gathered berries and seeds, and fished in nearby rivers and lakes. Those who lived on the Atlantic coast ate lots of shellfish!

They farmed, too. In the Northeast, corn, squash, and beans were three important crops called the "three sisters." Near the Great Lakes, native peoples farmed less because wild rice grew there.

After the "three sisters" were ready to be picked, they were eaten right away or dried for use during the winter.

TELL ME MORE

The northeastern part of North America has four seasons. The native peoples living there had to make sure they had enough food for winter when hunting and gathering were harder.

The MOHICAN

The Mohican (muh-HEE-kuhn) lived in the Hudson River valley in present-day New York State. Their name means "people of the waters that are never still."

The river was an important part of their life. People traveled along the river to fish, hunt, and fight. They made lightweight canoes from tree bark. One person could carry this type of canoe overland to get around dangerous waters. The Mohican also made large dugout canoes from tree trunks. These could carry many people.

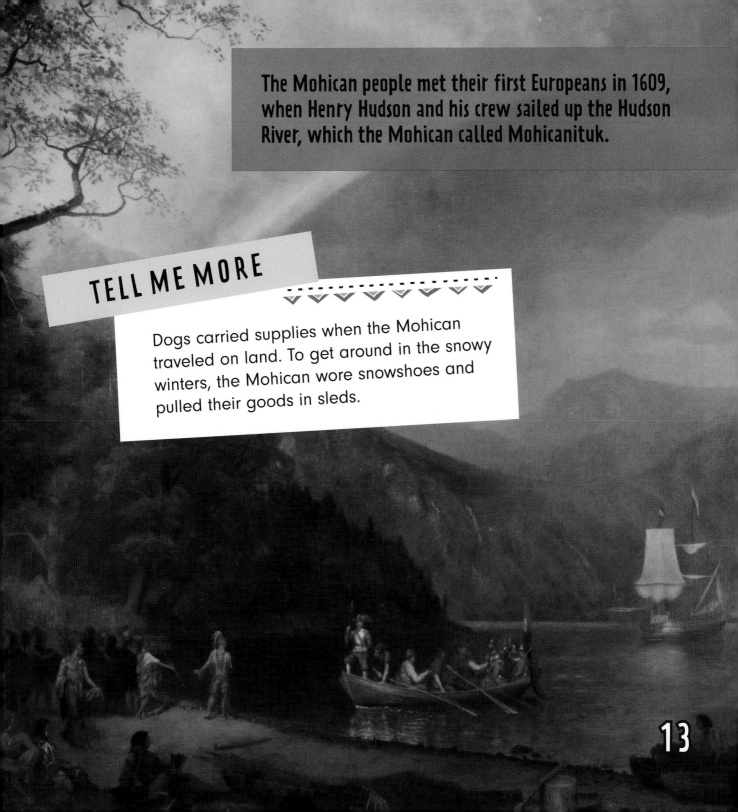

The Mohican people met their first Europeans in 1609, when Henry Hudson and his crew sailed up the Hudson River, which the Mohican called Mohicanituk.

TELL ME MORE

Dogs carried supplies when the Mohican traveled on land. To get around in the snowy winters, the Mohican wore snowshoes and pulled their goods in sleds.

The Iroquois CONFEDERACY

Centuries ago, the Cayuga, Mohawk, Oneida, Onondaga, and Seneca—and later the Tuscarora—formed a new and different type of government. Together, they've become known as the Iroquois **Confederacy**. The village chiefs of each group met and discussed ways to solve problems. Each group got one vote. All members had to agree before the confederacy would take action.

The confederacy members were peaceful with each other, but they often went to war with other groups. Because of their unity and government arrangement, they won many of these wars.

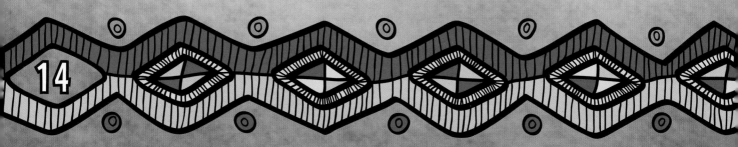

The Iroquois Confederacy was one of the largest and most powerful groups of native peoples in all North America.

TELL ME MORE

The people of the Iroquois Confederacy called themselves the Haudenosaunee (hoh-dee-noh-SHOH-nee), which meant "people of the longhouse."

The LENAPE (Delaware)

The Lenape (luh-NAH-pee) are one of the oldest of the native peoples in the Northeast. Many other groups called them "grandfathers" out of respect. Old stories say that many of the other northeastern peoples grew from the Lenape.

When the Europeans came to Lenape territory in modern New Jersey, they named the main river the Delaware. This was in honor of Lord De La Warr, an Englishman who helped found Virginia. They called the Lenape by the same name. Now the group goes by both names.

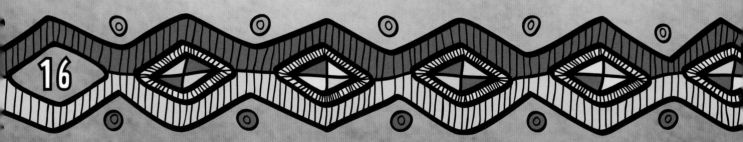

In Lenape **culture**, men, women, and children all had jobs to do and worked together to keep their people strong.

TELL ME MORE

The Lenape believed a spirit called the Mesingw (muh-SEENG) helped hunters find animals for food. Its scary face was red and black.

17

The Powhatan EMPIRE

The Powhatan empire was a collection of about 32 groups that lived along the Chesapeake Bay. One powerful ruler, named Wahunsonacock (wah-huhn-SEHN-uh-kawh), **conquered** and united the groups. He, his people, and his empire became known as Powhatan, named for his home village.

The groups all spoke Algonquian languages. Each group lived in several small villages that were located close to each other. A chief was in charge of each village. The chief made sure the people followed Powhatan's rules.

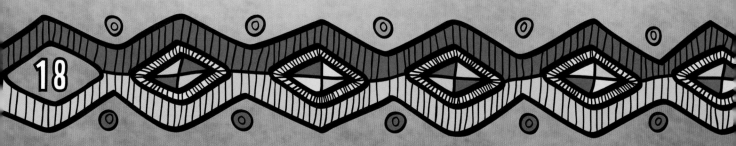

Pocahontas was Powhatan's daughter. Stories say she saved the life of an Englishman named John Smith, but that's likely untrue.

TELL ME MORE

Some of the groups in Powhatan's empire were the Mattaponi, Chickahominy, Nansemond, and Rappahannock.

The SHAWNEE

At first, the Shawnee lived in the Ohio River valley near the Iroquois. But the Iroquois forced the Shawnee to move south. They moved around a lot, mostly so they wouldn't have to fight with other native groups. But Shawnee warriors fought for their families if they were in danger.

By the mid-1700s, some Shawnee returned to Ohio. Settlers now lived on their land. Tecumseh was a famous Shawnee chief and warrior. He brought many native peoples together to try to win back Native American land.

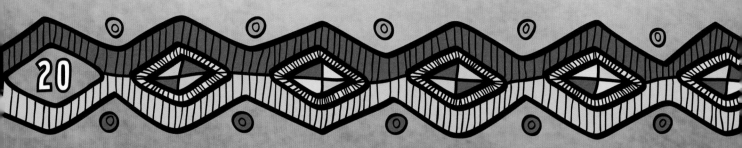

In the Shawnee language, "Tecumseh" means "shooting star" or "panther passing across the sky."

TELL ME MORE

Tecumseh died after fighting on the side of the British in the War of 1812, which was a war between the new United States and Great Britain that ended in 1815.

21

The Mystery of
CAHOKIA

On the edge of the northeastern region, archaeologists found the remains of a large, very old city in Illinois. It included 120 mounds made of earth! They called it Cahokia (kuh-HOH-kee-uh). They think an early native group known as the Mound Builders made it. Around 1100 to 1200, the city covered about 6 square miles (15.5 sq km) and was home to about 20,000 people.

Some of the mounds once had buildings on top of them. Other mounds were used for special occasions or burials.

Monk's Mound is the largest mound in North and South America. It's 100 feet (30.5 m) tall and almost 1,000 feet (305 m) long!

TELL ME MORE

The Mound Builders didn't have a written language. No one knows why the people of Cahokia left or where they went.

23

Europeans ARRIVE

Most native peoples of the Northeast first encountered European settlers during the 1600s. The Powhatan met colonists from the first successful English colony at Jamestown, Virginia, in 1607. As more colonies formed, the native groups lost more and more of their homelands. Many died fighting to stay, and even more died from European illnesses.

Then, in 1830, the US government forced all native groups to the western side of the Mississippi River. All their lands went to the settlers.

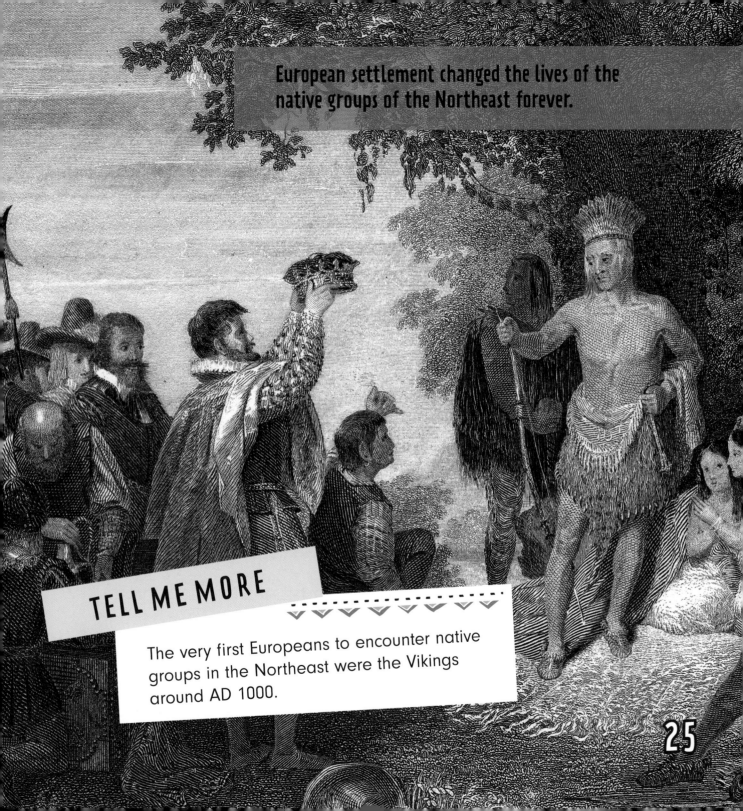

European settlement changed the lives of the native groups of the Northeast forever.

TELL ME MORE

The very first Europeans to encounter native groups in the Northeast were the Vikings around AD 1000.

Modern **TIMES**

Today, many **descendants** of northeastern native groups live on **reservations**, but they don't have to. Leaders work with the US government to better the lives of the northeastern native groups. Some schools on the reservations teach native languages and traditions.

Talented storytellers, artists, and musicians share their history and culture with their children and anyone else who wants to learn. Many groups hold **powwows** that are open to visitors. Native Americans visit schools and showcase their crafts at state and local fairs.

The native groups of the Northeast made beautiful art, which is often shown in museums in the area.

TELL ME MORE

Some of the northeastern peoples recognized by the US government are the Onondaga Nation, the Penobscot Nation, and the Wampanoag Tribe.

Native American WORDS

Did you know that some words we use come from the languages of the native peoples of North America? Here are just a few you might know!

animals	foods	rivers	clothes	things
chipmunk	chocolate	Erie	moccasin	canoe
moose	maize	Juniata	parka	kayak
muskrat	pecan	Potomac		hammock
opossum	squash	Susquehanna		
raccoon	succotash			

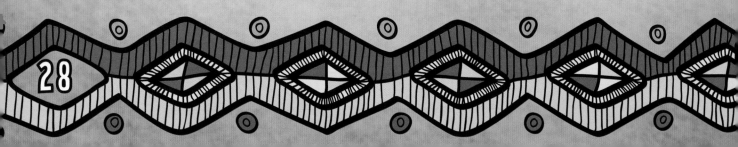

See which northeastern states have Native American names and what those names mean in English on this map!

Massachusetts
"great hill"

Wisconsin
"where waters gather"

Michigan
"great water"

Connecticut
"upon the long river"

Ohio
"beautiful valley"

Illinois
"men" or "great men"

TELL ME MORE

The common idea of "burying the hatchet," or making peace, comes from the Iroquois. To show they had made a peace agreement, they would actually bury hatchets, which are like axes, in the ground!

GLOSSARY

archaeologist: a person who digs up objects and remains of buildings to learn about life in the past

confederacy: two or more groups in an agreement of support

conquer: to take by force

council: a group of people meant to make decisions for a bigger group

culture: the beliefs and ways of life of a group of people

descendant: one who comes after others in a family

dome: a rounded roof, shaped like half of a sphere or globe

environment: the conditions that surround a living thing and affect the way it lives

permanent: meant to last a long time

powwow: a celebration of Native American ways of life, with songs and dances

region: a large area of land that has features that make it different from nearby areas of land

reservation: land set aside by the US government for Native Americans

stretch: to reach across

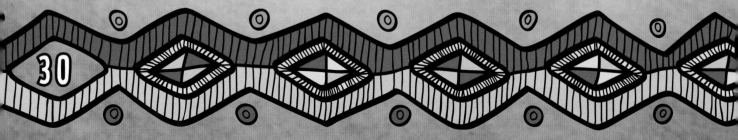

For More INFORMATION

Books

Ditchfield, Christin, *Northeast Indians*. Chicago, IL: Heinemann Library, 2012.

Hinton, Kaavonia. *The Iroquois of the Northeast.* Kennett Square, PA: Purple Toad Publishing, 2013.

National Museum of the American Indian. *Do All Indians Live in Tipis? Questions and Answers from the National Museum of the American Indian.* New York, NY: Collins, 2007.

Websites

National Museum of the American Indian
www.nmai.si.edu/

Take a virtual tour of the museum. Watch live webcasts and get links to films and other websites.

Native Americans for Kids: Northeast Woodland Indians in Olden Times
nativeamericans.mrdonn.org/northeast.html
Learn about the daily lives of the native peoples of the Northeast. Read some of their stories and myths.

INDEX